# THE SCOTTISH SONGS OF
# ROBERT BURNS

### 40 COMPLETE SONGS, COLLECTED, ARRANGED AND EDITED BY
## John Loesberg

**Ossian**
Cork
Edinburgh
Loughborough
New Hampshire

OSSIAN PUBLICATIONS LTD. IRELAND
(Publishing Dept.)
P.O. Box 84, Cork

OSSIAN PUBLICATIONS SCOTLAND
9 Rosebery Crescent
Edinburgh EH12 5JP

OSSIAN PUBLICATIONS U.K
Unit 3, Prince William Rd.
Loughborough

OSSIAN PUBLICATIONS USA
RR8 Box 374
Loudon, New Hampshire
03301

OMB 96
ISBN 0 946005 81 8

# Introduction

This small offering of forty of Robert Burns' songs is intended as an introduction to the man and his songs. Although Burns's work is read and loved all over the world, most of what is put forward tends to portray him as Burns the *Poet*. It goes without saying that indeed he was an extraordinarily fine, sensitive and witty lyrical poet, but is not the large body of songtexts he left us perhaps of even greater merit than his poetry and prose?

Much of Burns' literary work stemmed from the influences imposed upon him by the humble surroundings of his early years. Another profound source for much of his work comes from the folklore, superstitions and beliefs of the Scottish country people of the time. In particular Betty Davidson, an old woman who came to stay with the Burns family when Robert was only ten years of age, helped him to develop a powerfully imaginative use of the language, through her wealth of stories and songs.

It may be said that in Burns' times, just like today, song-lyrics were the poetry of the common people. A nation such as Scotland, with its farmers, fishermen, craftsmen and labourers, would have had few literate citizens in the 18th century. Nevertheless, and in spite of a lack of education and books, the 'plain folk' had inherited an incredible wealth of poetry and sheer power of words, inspiring and moving them.

Of course right through history we may observe how 'plain folk' created virtually all the origins of language, song, dance, cuisine etc. It was only when the gentry stylized any of these 'basic' ideas that they started to claim them as 'theirs' and believed themselves to be cultured.

In any case, the memorising of poems and songs has been part and parcel of Scottish popular culture since time immemorial.

A most unusual aspect of Burns is the fact that although it would have been tempting perhaps to any other contemporary poet, he hardly ever corrupted the original and traditional lyrics and songs of the people. Although he may have dabbled in some fashionable 'art' songs (as did Thomas Moore, the Irish poet, around the same time) the greater part of his output is true to the traditional character of Scottish song.

It is here that we must pause and realise the enormous and difficult task Burns undertook when he nearly single-handedly set out to write down and preserve so many traditional Scottish songs. The notion, of course, of collecting folksongs is a fairly recent one and it took another century before serious-minded collectors travelled the highways and byways of the country to listen to the people and their songs.

OMB 96

It is to Burns' eternal credit that virtually all the songs and fragments of songs he collected were lovingly restored to new, singable versions. At other times he would just compose an entirely new song, but completely in keeping with traditional Scottish song both textually and musically.

It has been estimated that Burns collected and wrote no less than 400 songs. A great many of these were first published between 1786 and 1803 in publications by the Edinburgh printer James Johnson - '*The Scots Musical Museum*' (six volumes). Later on Burns contributed to George Thomson's '*Select Melodies of Scotland*'. Both these publications were instant successes for Burns and his publishers who appeared to have produced the songs in the right place and at the right time, when the nation was undergoing a re-appraisal of Scottish nationalism, albeit in a fairly un-political way.

Although it may be said that in general Burns' way of re-writing or completing these songs was extremely successful and upheld all norms of musical integrity, he did slip occasionally. Old songs such as 'Barbara Allen', 'Dainty Davie', and 'MacPherson's Farewell' suffered some 'improvements' at his hands, which even in his time people would have rejected as too stilted. On the other hand, when comparing a full set of words of a traditional song such as 'To Daunton Me' next to Burns's version of the same song, it becomes clear that his sense of metrical balance, his deep understanding of the rhythm of the song makes it easily the better of the two.

One wonders would Scotland still be Scotland without songs such as 'Scots Wha Hae', 'A Man's A Man for All That' and 'Auld Lang Syne'? What's more - will the world ever again see the like of a poet who gave his verses such a universality that still strikes a chord two hundred years later?

> Then let us pray that come what may,
> As come it will for a' that
> That Sense and Worth, o'er a' the earth,
> May bear the gree*, and a' that,
> It's comin' yet for a' that.
> That Man to Man, the world o'er,
> Shall Brothers be for a' that!

For further reading, a bibliography may be found on page 71 but for some excellent introductions to Robert Burns look no further than the following unpretentious and well-written book(let)s:

*Poems and songs of Robert Burns* by Nancy Marshall, Chambers, Edinburgh 1991 (no music included)

*Robert Burns' Scotland*, by Rev. J.A. Carruth, Jarrold & Sons Ltd., Norwich 1986

---

* gree — be victorious

# A NOTE ON THE SONGS

An extensive search was made for the original of each song, often resulting in as many as six (slightly different) versions. The bibliography in the back of this book will show the sources used. In some cases repeated inconsistencies or corrupted lyrics were detected and corrected.

The guitar accompaniments are basic in most cases, occasionally a better fitting chord is introduced - especially in the slower songs. The use of the dominant seventh has been greatly restricted - a personal whim, I'm afraid! To preserve the strength of the original, plain melodies I felt it advisable to leave out as many 7th chords as possible. In fact a lot of folkmusic would gain by not suffering the inclusion of this mainly 19th century notion of using this type of chord. It often creates a feeling of tension and expectation at certain passages that most songs can do without.

The ability to use a capo for changing the pitch of the guitar is very much recommended, as is some basic knowledge of transposing the key of a song if found unsuitable. Forcing one's voice, when it's clear that the key should be changed, is not a viable solution. Why squeak or grunt when it can be done differently?

The music throughout this book has been engraved in such a way as to make it easy to read both for singers as well as for instrumentalists. This means that most of the semiquavers are beamed together making the score look much less cluttered and much more comprehensible for singers and instrumentalists alike. Some more songs of Burns may be found in three other titles in this range: *Traditional Folksongs and Ballads of Scotland*, Vols. 1, 2, & 3.

John Loesberg

OMB 96

## A WORD ON THE LOWLANDS SCOTS LANGUAGE

Burns' language was that of his native Scots dialect, a language riddled with expressive words, many of which can be found in the songs. Although a good many of these words may be readily understood, some need explanation.

The more unusual Scots dialect words are explained in the 'Brief Guide to the Songs' section at the back of the book.

The Scots tongue, or Braid Scots, is a rich amalgam of old English plus many words and expressions taken on board as a result of historical incursions, political alliances and trade connections. One must remember that up to about two hundred years ago it would have been relatively easier for the Scots to travel by water to Scandinavia, the Netherlands and other places than to reach London by sea or by road*. Scandinavian influences may be found in abundant measure in the North East and the Shetland and Orkney Islands, while Dutch and Flemish fishermen and craftsmen always had a foothold along many parts of the Eastern seaboard. Equally, Scots sailors and merchants had their bases on the continent, travelled as far as France and Spain on a regular basis and especially when the political situation necessitated this, ties with places other than England were strengthened. Many verbs and nouns may be found in Lowland Scots that appear closer to the West Germanic languages, in particular Scandinavian and Dutch while other words have a distinctive French origin.

As an example of how tenuous the foothold of Scottish/Continental trade was it is interesting to see that since the 14th century and lasting until the end of the 18th century Scottish merchants and their families were established in the Netherlands and had their own Scots-Presbyterian and Episcopalian churches in some of the ports. (As a linguistic aside it is interesting to note how the Dutch word for church 'kerk'** must have given rise to the 'kirk' - the name of the Calvinist faith of Scotland). In the 17th century the trading centre of Rotterdam boasted a fleet of 100 vessels which plied trade solely with Scotland. Another language link may be seen in the use of diminutives in Scotland which is quite similar to that of present-day Dutch - wifie/wijfje; housie/huisje; pinkie/pinkie - (little finger)

---

\* in the year 1750 the speediest journey time between Edinburgh and London using Turnpike roads was 230 hours of continuous (and bumpy) travel.

\*\* 'kirche' in German
'kirkja' in Old Norse

6

Here follow some other examples of foreign words that in Burns's days would have been common enough - note the significant differences from the English sounds.

| Scots | Norse | English |
|-------|-------|---------|
| frae | frae | from |
| gate | gatan | road |
| gowk | gauk | a fool |
| bairn | barn | child |

| Scots | French | English |
|-------|--------|---------|
| sussy | souci | trouble/worry |
| disjune | (petit) dejeuner | breakfast |
| tassie | tasse | cup |
| ashet | assiette | plate |

| Scots | Dutch | English |
|-------|-------|---------|
| mutch | muts | cap |
| host | hoest | cough |
| cuit | kuit | ankle |

For further reading :
*The Guid Scots Tongue*, by David Murison, The Mercat Press, Edinburgh 1977
*The Concise Scots Dictionary*, edited by Mairi Robinson, Aberdeen University Press, 1985.

OMB 96

' That I for poor old Scotland's sake
some useful plan or book could make
or sing a sang at least.'

Robert Burns

# Scots, Wha Hae

♩ = 66

Scots, wha hae wi' Wal- lace bled, Scots,wham Bruce has af- ten led,

Wel-come to your go- ry bed, Or to vic- to- rie !

Now's the day, and now's the hour; See the front o' bat- tle lour;

See ap-proach proud Ed- ward's pow'r, Chains and sla- ve- rie !

Wha will be a traitor knave ?
Wha can fill a coward's grave ?
Wha sae base as be a slave ?
       Let him turn and flee !
Wha, for Scotland's King and Law,
Freedom's sword will strongly draw,
Freeman stand, or Freeman fa',
       Let him on wi' me !

By Oppression's woes and pains !
By your sons in servile chains !
We will drain our dearest veins,
       But they shall be free !
Lay the proud Usurpers low !
Tyrants fall in every foe !
Liberty's in every blow !

       Let us do or die !

OMB 96

# O Whistle an' I'll Come to You

At kirk, or at market, whene'er ye meet me,
Gang by me as tho' that ye car'd na a flie;
But steal me a blink o' your bonnie black e'e,
Yet look as ye were na lookin to me,
Yet look as ye were na lookin to me.

Aye vow and protest that ye care na for me,
And whiles ye may lightly my beauty a-wee;
But court na anither, tho' jokin ye be,
For fear that she wile your fancy frae me,
For fear that she wile your fancy frae me.

*Chorus*

*Chorus*

# Craigieburn Wood

Fain, fain would I my griefs impart,
Yet dare na for your anger;
But secret love will break my heart.
If I conceal it langer.
If thou refuse to pity me,
If thou shalt love anither,
When yon green leaves fade frae the tree,
Around my grave they'll wither.

OMB 96

# The Gloomy Night

The Autumn mourns her rip'ning corn
By early Winter's ravage torn;
Across her placid, azure sky
She sees the scowling tempest fly:
Chill runs my blood to hear it rave.
I think upon the stormy wave,
Where many a danger I must dare,
Far from the bonnie banks of Ayr.

'Tis not the surging billows roar,
'Tis not that fatal, deadly shore;
Tho' Death in ev'ry shape appear,
The wretched have no more to fear:
But round my heart the ties are bound,
That heart transpierc'd with many a wound;
These bleed afresh those ties I tear,
To leave the bonnie banks of Ayr.

Farewell old Coila's hills and dales,
Her heathy moors and winding vales;
The scenes where wretched fancy roves,
Pursuing past, unhappy loves !
Farewell, my friends, farewell my foes,
My peace with these, my love with those;
The bursting tears my heart declare;
Farewell the bonnie banks of Ayr.

OMB 96

# My Tocher's the Jewel

♩. = 80

O mei-kle thinks my love o' my beau-ty, And mei-kle thinks my love o' my kin; But lit-tle thinks my love I ken braw-lie, My toch-er's the jew-el has charms for him, It's a' for the ap-ple he'll nou-rish the tree, It's a' for the hin-ey he'll che-rish the bee; My lad-die's sae mei-kle in love wi' the sil-ler, He can-na hae love to spare for me.

Your proffer o' love's an airle-penny,
My tocher's the bargain ye wad buy;
But an ye be crafty, I am cunnin,
Sae wi' anither your fortune maun try.
Ye're like to the timmer ' yon rotten wood,
Ye're like to the bark o' yon rotten tree,
Ye'll slip frae me like a knotless thread,
And ye'll crack your credit wi' mair nor me.

# To the Weavers Gin Ye Go

♩ = 100

My heart was ance as blythe and free As sim-mer days were lang; But a bon- nie, west- lin' wea- ver lad, Has gart me change my sang. To the wea- vers gin ye go, fair maid, To the wea- vers gin ye go, I rede ye right, gang ne'er at night, To the wea- vers gin ye go.

2 A bonnie, westlin weaver lad
Sat working at his loom;
He took my heart as wi' a net,
In every knot and thrum.

*Chorus*

3 I sat beside my warpin-wheel,
And aye I ca'd it roun';
But every shot and every knock,
My heart it gae a stoun.

*Chorus*

4 The moon was sinking in the west,
Wi' visage pale and wan,
And my bonnie, westlin weaver lad
Convoy'd me thro' the glen.

*Chorus*

5 But what was said, or what was done,
Shame fa' me gin I tell;
But Oh ! I fear the kintra soon
Will ken as weel's mysel !

*Chorus*

OMB 96

# Highland Mary

How sweetly bloom'd the gay, green birk,
How rich the hawthorn's blossom,
As underneath their fragrant shade,
I clasp'd her to my bosom !
The golden Hours on angel wings,
Flew o'er me and my dearie;
For dear to me, as light and life,
Was my sweet Highland Mary.

Wi' mony a vow, and lock'd embrace,
Our parting was fu' tender;
And, pledging aft to meet again,
We tore oursels asunder;
But O, fell Death's untimely frost,
That nipt my flower sae early !
Now green's the sod, and cauld's the clay
That wraps my Highland Mary !

O pale, pale now, those rosy lips,
I aft hae kiss'd sae fondly !
And clos'd for aye, the sparkling glance
That dwalt on me sae kindly !
And mouldering now in silent dust,
That heart that lo'ed me dearly !
But still within my bosom's core
Shall live my Highland Mary.

OMB 96

# My Love She's but a Lassie Yet

♩ = 88

Chorus

My love she's but a las-sie yet, My love she's but a las-sie yet; We'll let her stand a year or twa, She'll no be half sae sau-cy yet. I rue the day I sought her, O, I rue the day I sought her, O. Wha gets her needs na say she's woo'd, but he may say he's bought her, O !

Come draw a drap o' the best o't yet,
Come draw a drap o' the best o't yet,
Gae seek for pleasure whare you will,
But here I never miss'd it yet.

*Chorus*

We're a' dry wi' drinkin o't,
We're a' dry wi' drinkin o't;
The minister kiss'd the fiddler's wife;
He could na preach for thinkin o't.

*Chorus*

# The Gallant Weaver

♩ = 132

Where Cart rins row- in' to the sea, By mo-ny a flow'r and spread- ing tree, There lives a lad, the lad for me, He is a gal- lant Wea- ver, Oh, I had woo- ers aught or nine, They gied me rings and rib- bons fine; And I was fear'd my heart wad tine, And I gied it to the Wea- ver.

My daddie sign'd my tocher-band,
To gie the lad that has the land,
But to my heart I'll add my hand,
And give it to the Weaver.
While birds rejoice in leafy bowers,
While bees delight in opening flowers,
While corn grows green in summer showers,
I love my gallant Weaver.

OMB 96

# Last May, a Braw Wooer

He spak o' the darts in my bonnie black e'en,
And vow'd for my love he was diein,
I said, he might die when he liked for Jean —
The Lord forgie me for liein, for liein;
The Lord forgie me for liein !

A weel-stocked mailen, himsel' for the laird,
And marriage aff-hand, were his proffers;
I never loot on that I kenn'd it, or car'd;
But thought I might hae waur offers, waur offers,
But thought I might hae waur offers.

But what wad ye think ?—in a fortnight or less
(The deil tak his taste to gae near her !)
He up the Gate-slack to my black cousin, Bess —
Guess ye how, the jad ! I could bear her, could bear her,
Guess ye how, the jad ! I could bear her.

But a' the niest week, as I petted wi' care,
I gaed to the tryst o' Dalgarnock;
But wha but my fine fickle wooer was there,
I glowr'd as I'd seen a warlock, a warlock,
I glowr'd as I'd seen a warlock.

But owre my left shouther I gae him a blink,
Lest neibours might say I was saucy;
My wooer he caper'd as he'd been in drink,
And vow'd I was his dear lassie, dear lassie,
And vow'd I was his dear lassie.

I spier'd for my cousin fu' couthy and sweet,
Gin she had recover'd her hearin,
And how her new shoon fit her auld schachl't feet;
But heavens ! how he fell a swearing, a swearing,
But heavens ! how he fell as swearing.

He begged for gudesake, I wad be his wife,
Or else I wad kill him wi' sorrow;
So e'en to preserve the poor body in life,
I think I maun wed him to-morrow, to-morrow,
I think I maun wed him to-morrow.

# Gae Bring to me a Pint o' Wine

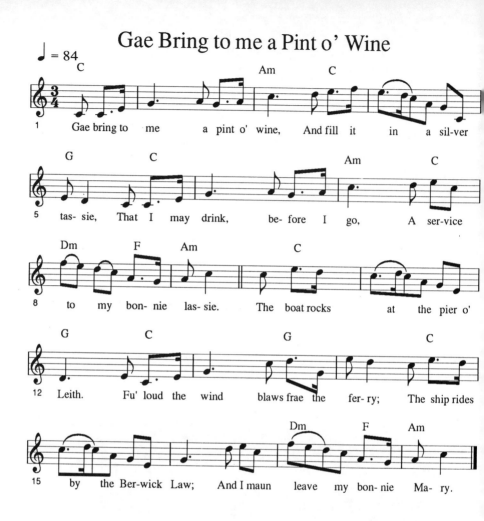

The trumpets sound, the banners fly
The glittering spears are ranked ready;
The shouts o' war are heard afar,
The battle closes deep and bloody !
It's not the roar o' sea or shore
Wad make' me langer wish to tarry,
Nor shouts o' war that's heard afar,
It's leaving thee, my bonnie Mary.

# Ye Banks and Braes

Aft hae I rov'd by Bonnie Doon,
To see the rose and woodbine twine:
And ilka bird sang o' its luve,
And fondly sae did I o' mine.
Wi' lightsome heart I pu'd a rose,
Fu' sweet upon its thorny tree !
And my fause luver staw my rose,
But ah ! he left the thorn wi' me.

OMB 96

# O This is No My Ain Lassie

*Chorus*

She's bonnie, blooming, straight, and tall,
And lang has had my heart in thrall;
And aye it charms my very saul,
The kind love that's in her e'e.

*Chorus*

A thief sae pawkie is my Jean,
To steal a blink, by a' unseen;
But gleg as light are lover's e'en,
When kind love is in the e'e.

*Chorus*

It may escape the courtly sparks,
It may escape the learned clerks;
But well the watching lover marks
The kind love that's in her e'e.

*Chorus*

# The Birks of Aberfeldy

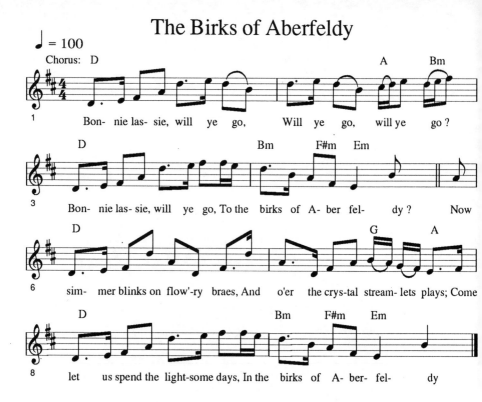

*Chorus*

2 The little birdies blythely sing,
  While o'er their heads the hazels hing,
  Or lightly flit on wanton wing
  In the birks of Aberfeldy.

*Chorus*

3 The braes ascend like lofty wa's,
  The foamy stream deep-roaring fa's,
  O'erhung wi' fragrant spreading shaws
  The birks of Aberfeldy

*Chorus*

4 The hoary cliffs are crown'd wi' flowers,
  White o'er the linns the burnie pours,
  And rising, weets wi' misty showers
  The birks of Aberfeldy.

*Chorus*

5 Let Fortune's gifts at random flee,
  They ne'er shall draw a wish frae me;
  Supremely blest wi' love and thee,
  In the birks of Aberfeldy.

*Chorus*

# Lord Gregory

Lord Gregory, mind'st thou not the grove
By bonnie Irwine side,
Where first I own'd that virgin love
I lang, lang had denied.
How aften didst thou pledge and vow
Thou wad for aye be mine !
And my fond heart, itsel' sae true,
It ne'er mistrusted thine.

Hard is thy heart, Lord Gregory,
And flinty is thy breast:
Thou bolt of Heaven that flashest by,
O, wilt thou bring me rest !
Ye mustering thunders from above,
Your willing victim see;
But spare and pardon my fause Love
His wrangs to Heaven and me.

OMB 96

# O Willie Brew'd a Peck o' Maut

Here are we met, three merry boys,
Three merry boys I trow are we;
And mony a night we've merry been,
And mony mair we hope to be !

*Chorus*

It is the moon, I ken her horn,
That's blinkin' in the lift sae hie;
She shines sae bright to wile us hame,
But, by my sooth, she'll wait a wee !

*Chorus*

Wha first shall rise to gang awa,
A cuckold, coward loun is he !
Wha first beside his chair shall fa',
He is the King amang us three.

*Chorus*

OMB 96

# My Love is Like a Red, Red Rose

♩ = 76

O, my love is like a red, red rose, That's new- ly sprung in June; O, my

love is like the me- lo- die that's sweet- ly play'd in tune. As

fair art thou, my bon-nie lass, so deep in luve am I; And

I will luve thee still, my dear, till a' the seas gang dry, Till

a' the seas gang dry, my dear, till a' the seas gang dry, And

I will luve thee still, my dear, till a' the seas gang dry.

Till a' the seas gang dry, my dear,
And the rocks melt wi' the sun;
And I will luve thee still, my dear,
While the sands o' life shall run.

And fare-thee-weel, my only luve !
And fare-thee-weel a while !
And I will come again, my luve,
Tho' it were ten thousand mile.

# She's Fair and Fause

♩. = 66

Whae'er ye be that woman love,
To this be never blind;
Nae ferlie 'tis tho' fickle she prove,
A woman has't by kind.
O Woman lovely, Woman fair !
An angel form's fa'n to thy share,
'Twad been o'er meikle to gi'en thee mair —
I mean an angel mind

OMB 96

# Tam Glen

There's Lowrie the Laird o' Dumeller—
'Gude day to you, brute !' he comes ben.
He brags and he blaws o' his siller,
But when will he dance like Tam Glen !

My minnie does constantly deave me,
And bids me beware o' young men;
They flatter, she says, to deceive me, —
But wha can think sae o' Tam Glen !

My daddie says, gin I'll forsake him,
He'd gie me gude hunder marks ten;
But, if it's ordain'd I maun take him,
O wha will I get but Tam Glen !

Yestreen at the valentines' dealing,
My heart to my mou' gied a sten';
For thrice I drew ane without failing,
And thrice it was written 'Tam Glen" !

The last Halloween I was waukin
My droukit sark-sleeve, as ye ken,
His likeness came up the house staukin,
And the very grey breeks o' Tam Glen !

Come, counsel, dear tittie, don't tarry;
I'll gie ye my bonnie black hen,
Gif ye will advise me to marry
The lad I lo'e dearly, Tam Glen.

33

# My Wife's a Winsome Wee Thing

**Chorus**

The warld's wrack, we share o't,
The warstle and the care o't;
Wi' her I'll blythely bear it,
And think my lot divine.

# My Heart's in the Highlands

$\quad \cdot = 96$

My heart's in the High-lands, my heart is not here, My heart's in the High-lands, a- chas-ing the deer; A- cha-sing the wild deer, and fol-low-ing the roe, My heart's in the High-lands wher-e- ver I go.

Farewell to the Highlands, farewell to the North,
The birth-place of Valour, the country of Worth;
Wherever I wander, wherever I rove,
The hills of the Highlands for ever I love.

Farewell to the mountains, high-cover'd with snow,
Farewell to the straths and green valleys below;
Farewell to the forests and wild-hanging woods,
Farewell to the torrents and loud-pouring floods.

My heart's in the Highlands, my heart is not here,
My heart's in the Highlands, a-chasing the deer;
A-chasing the wild deer, and following the roe,
My heart's in the Highlands wherever I go.

OMB 96

# The Deil's Awa' wi' th'Exciseman

The deil cam' fid- dlin' through the toun and danc'd a- wa' wi' th'ex-
cise man; And il- ka auld wife cried, 'Auld ma- houn, I
wish you luck o' the prize, man'. The deil's a- wa', the
deil's a- wa', the deil's a- wa' wi' th'ex- cise- man; he's
danc'd a- wa', he's danc'd a- wa,' he's danc'd a-wa' wi' th'ex-cise- man.

We'll mak our maut, and we'll brew our drink,
We'll laugh, sing, and rejoice, man,
And mony braw thanks to the meikle black deil,
That danc'd awa wi' th' Exciseman.

*Chorus*

There's threesome reels, there's foursome reels,
There's hornpipes and strathspeys, man,
But the ae best dance ere came to the land
Was 'The deil's awa wi' the' Exciseman.'

*Chorus*

# What can a Young Lassie do wi' an Auld Man ?

♩. = 80

He's always compleenin frae mornin to e'enin,
He hosts and he hirples the weary day lang;
He's doylt and he's dozin, his blude it is frozen,—
O dreary's the night wi' a crazy auld man !

*Chorus*

He hums and he hankers, he frets and he cankers,
I never can please him do a' that I can;
He's peevish and jealous o' a' the young fellows,—
O dool on the day I met wi' an auld man !

*Chorus*

My auld auntie Katie upon me taks pity,
I'll do her endeavour to follow her plan;
I'll cross him an' wrack him, until I heartbreak him
And then his auld brass will buy me a new pan !

OMB 96

# There was a Lad was Born in Kyle

Our Monarch's hindmost year but ane
Was five-and-twenty days begun,
'Twas then a blast o'Janwar' win'
Blew hansel in on Robin.

*Chorus*

The gossip keekit in his loof,
Quo' scho, 'Wha lives will see the proof,
This waly boy will be nae coof:
I think we'll ca' him Robin.'

*Chorus*

'He'll hae misfortunes great an' sma',
But aye a heart aboon them a'.
He'll be a credit to us a':
We'll a' be proud o' Robin.'

*Chorus*

'But sure as three times three mak nine,
I see by ilka score and line,
This chap will dearly like our kin',
So leeze me on thee ! Robin !'

*Chorus*

'Guid faith, quo' scho, 'I doubt you, sir,
Ye gar the lasses lie aspar;
But twenty fauts ye may hae waur,
So blessins on thee, Robin !'

BIRTH PLACE OF BURNS.

OMB 96

# The Highland Widow's Lament

♩ = 108

O, I am come to the Low Coun- trie, Ochon, och- on, och- rie; With- out a pen- ny
in my purse, to buy a meal to me.

2. It was na sae in the Highland hills,
   Ochon, Ochon, Ochrie !
   Nae woman in the country wide,
   Sae happy was as me.

3. For then I had a score o' kye,
   Ochon, Ochon, Ochrie !
   Feeding on yon hill sae high,
   And giving milk to me.

4. And there I had three score o' yowes,
   Ochon, Ochon, Ochrie !
   Skipping on yon bonnie knowes,
   And casting woo to me.

5. I was the happiest of a' the Clan,
   Sair, sair, may I repine;
   For Donald was the brawest man,
   And Donald he was mine.

6. Till Charlie Stewart cam at last,
   Sae far to set us free;
   My Donald's arm was wanted then,
   For Scotland and for me.

7. Their waefu' fate what need I tell,
   Right to the wrang did yield;
   My Donald and his country fell,
   Upon Culloden field.

8. Ochon ! O Donald, oh !
   Ochon, Ochon, Ochrie !
   Nae woman in warld wide,
   Sae wretched now as me.

# Wandering Willie

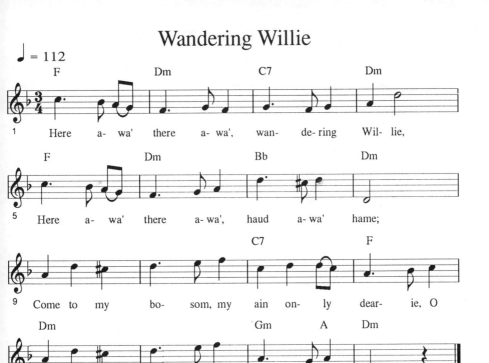

Winter winds blew loud and cauld at our parting,
Fears for my Willie brought tears in my e'e:
Welcome now simmer, and welcome my Willie,
The simmer to nature, my Willie to me.

Rest, ye wild storms, in the cave of your slumbers,
How your dread howling a lover alarms !
Wauken, ye breezes, row gently ye billows,
And waft my dear laddie ance mair to my arms.

But oh, if he's faithless, and minds na his Nannie,
Flow still between us thou wide-roaring main;
May I never see it, may I never trow it,
But, dying, believe that my Willie's my ain.

OMB 96

# A Highland Lad my Love was Born

With his philibeg an' tartan plaid,
An' gude claymore down by his side,
The ladies hearts he did trepan,
My gallant braw John Highlandman.

*Chorus*

We ranged a' from Tweed to Spey,
An' liv'd like lords and ladies gay;
For a Lalland face he feared nane,
My gallant braw John Highlandman.

*Chorus*

They banish'd him beyond the sea,
But ere the bud was on the tree
Adown my cheeks the pearls ran,
Embracing my John Highlandman.

*Chorus*

But oh ! they catched him at last
And bound him in a dungeon fast;
My curse upon them every one:
They've hang'd my braw John Highlandman.

*Chorus*

And now a widow, I must mourn,
The pleasures that shall ne'er return;
No comfort but a hearty cann,
When I think on John Highlandman.

*Chorus*

43

# Whistle o'er the Lave o't

First when Mag-gie was my care, Heav'n, I thought was in her air;

Now we're mar-ried spier nae mair, But whist-le o'er the lave o't!

Meg was meek, and Meg was mild, Sweet and harm-less as a child –

Wi- ser men than me's be- guil'd; Sae whist-le o'er the lave o't!

How we live, my Meg and me,
How we love, and how we gree,
I care na by how few may see —
Whistle o'er the lave o't !
Wha I wish were maggot's meat,
Dish'd up in her winding sheet,
I could write— but Meg maun see't —
Whistle o'er the lave o't !

# A Rosebud by my Early Walk

♩. = 80

A Rose-bud by my ear- ly walk, A- down a corn en-closed bank Sae gent- ly bent its thorn- y stalk, All on a dew- y morn- ing. Ere twice the shades o' dawn are fled, In a' its crim- son glo- ry spread, And droop- ing rich the dew- y head, It scents the ear- ly morn- ing.

Within the bush her covert nest
A little linnet fondly prest;
The dew sat chilly on her breast,
    Sae early in the morning.
She soon shall see her tender brood,
The pride, the pleasure o' the wood,
Amang the fresh green leaves bedew'd,
    Awake the early morning.

So thou, dear bird, young Jeany fair,
On trembling string or vocal air,
Shall sweetly pay the tender care
    That tents thy early morning.
So thou, sweet Rose-bud, young and gay,
Shalt beauteous blaze upon the day,
And bless the parent's evening ray
    That watch'd thy early morning.

OMB 96

# A Man's a Man for a' That

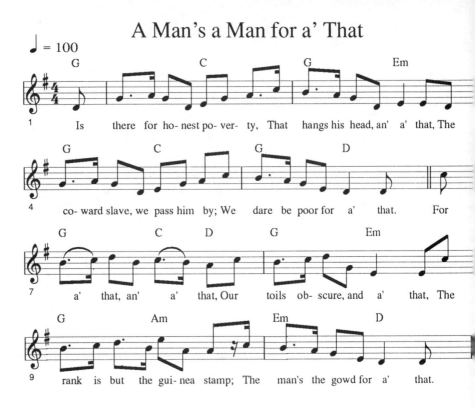

♩ = 100

What though on hamely fare we dine,
Wear hoddin grey, an a' that ?
Gie fools their silks, and knaves their wine,
A man's a man for a' that.
For a' that, an' a' that,
Their tinsel show, an' a' that,
The honest man, tho' e'er sae poor,
Is king o' men for a' that.

Ye see yon birkie ca'd a lord,
Wha struts, an' stares, an' a' that;
Tho' hundreds worship at his word,
He's but a coof for a' that.
For a' that, an' a' that,
His ribband, star, an' a' that,
The man of independent mind
He looks an' laughs at a' that.

A prince can mak a belted knight,
A marquis, duke, an' a' that;
But an honest man's aboon his might,
Gude faith, he maunna fa' that !
For a' that, an' a' that,
Their dignities an' a' that,
The pith o' sense, an' pride o' worth,
Are higher rank than a' that.

Then let us pray that come it may,
(As come it will for a' that)
That Sense and Worth, o'er a' the earth,
Shall bear the gree, an' a' that.
For a' that, a' a' that,
It's coming yet for a' that,
That man to man, the world o'er,
Shall brithers be for a' that.

OMB 96

# Ae Fond Kiss

1    Ae fond kiss and   then we se- ver!   Ae   fare-well and   then   for- e- ver!

5    Deep in heart-wrung tears I'll pledge thee,   war-ring sighs and grooms I'll wage thee.

I'll ne'er blame my partial fancy,
Naething could resist my Nancy:
But to see her was to love her;
Love but her, and love for ever.
had we never lov'd sae kindly,
Had we never lov'd sae blindly,
Never met — or never parted,
We had ne'er been broken-hearted.

Fare-thee-weel, thou first and fairest!
Fare-the-weel, thou best and dearest!
Thine be ilka joy and treasure,
Peace, Enjoyment. Love and Pleasure!
Ae fond kiss, and then we sever!
Ae fareweel, alas, for ever!
Deep in heart-wrung tears I'll pledge thee,
Warring sighs and groans I'll wage thee.

# Braw, Braw Lads

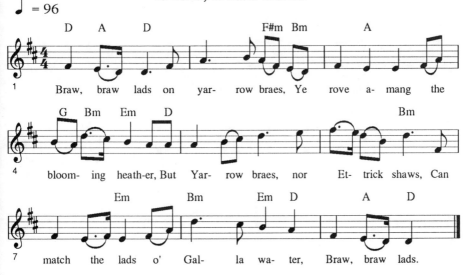

♩ = 96

Braw, braw lads on yar- row braes, Ye rove a- mang the

bloom- ing heath-er, But Yar- row braes, nor Et- trick shaws, Can

match the lads o' Gal- la wa- ter, Braw, braw lads.

But there is ane, a secret ane,
Aboon them a' I lo'e him better;
And I'll be his, and he'll be mine,
The bonnie lad o' Galla Water,
Braw, braw lads.

Altho' his daddie was nae laird,
And tho' I hae nae meikle tocher,
Yet rich in kindest, truest love,
We'll tent our flocks by Galla Water,
Braw, braw lads.

It ne'er was wealth, it ne'er was wealth,
That coft contentment, peace, or pleasure:
The bands and bliss o' mutual love,
O that's the chiefest world's treasure,
Braw, braw lads.

OMB 96

# Bonnie Jean

♩ = 112

There was a lass and she was fair, At kirk and mar- ket to be seen, When a' the fair- est maids were met, The fair- est maid was bon- nie Jean. And aye she wrought her mam- my's wark, And aye she sang sae mer- ri- lie; The blyth- est bird up- on the bush. Had ne'er a light- er heart than she.

3  But hawks will rob the tender joys
   That bless the little lintwhite's nest;
   And frost will blight the fairest flowers,
   And love will break the soundest rest.

4  Young Robbie was the brawest lad,
   The flower and pride of a' the glen;
   And he had owsen, sheep, and kye,
   And wanton naigies nine or ten.

5  He gaed wi' Jeanie to the tryste,
   He danc'd wi' Jeanie on the down;
   And, lang ere witless Jeanie wist,
   Her heart was tint, her peace was stown !

6  As in the bosom of the stream,
   The moon-beam dwells at dewy e'en;
   So trembling pure was tender love
   Within the breast of bonnie Jean.

7  And now she works her mammy's wark,
   And aye she sighs wi' care and pain;
   Yet wist na what her il might be,
   Or what wad make her weel again.

8  But didna Jeanie's heart loup light,
   And didna joy blink in her e'e,
   As Robbie tauld a tale o' love
   Ae e'ening on the lily lea ?

9  The sun was sinking in the west,
   The birds sang sweet in ilka grove;
   His cheek to hers he fondly laid,
   And whisper'd thus his tale o' love:

10 'O Jeanie fair, I lo'e thee dear;
   O canst thou think to fancy me,
   Or wilt thou leave thy mammie's cot,
   And learn to tent the farms wi' me ?

11 'At barn or byre thou shalt na drudge,
   Or naething else to trouble thee;
   But stray amang the heather-bells,
   And tent the waving corn wi' me.'

12 Now what could artless Jeanie do ?
   She had nae will to say him na:
   At length she blush'd a sweet consent,
   And love was aye between then twa.

OMB 96

# Ay Waukin' O !

*Chorus*

When I sleep I dream,
When I wauk I'm eerie;
Sleep I can get nane
For thinking on my dearie.

*Chorus*

Lanely night comes on
A' the lave are sleepin';
I think on my bonnie lad,
And I bleer my e'en wi' greetin'.

*Chorus*

# Comin' Thro' the Rye

2. Gin a body meet a body
   Comin' frae the town;
   Gin a body greet a body,
   Need a body frown ?
   Ilka lassie has her laddie,
   Nane, they say, ha'e I !
   But a' the lads they lo'e me weel,
   An' what the waur am I ?

3. Gin a body meet a body
   Comin' from the well;
   Gin a body kiss a body
   Need a body tell ?
   Ilka lassie has her laddie,
   Ne'er a ane ha'e I;
   But a' the lads they smile on me
   When comin' thro' the rye.

4. Amang the train there is a swain
   I dearly lo'e mysel';
   But what his name, or where his hame,
   I dinna care to tell.
   Ilka lassie has her laddie,
   Nane, they say ha'e I,
   Yet a' the lads they smile at me
   When comin' thro' the rye.

OMB 96

# Corn Rigs are Bonnie

hap- py night, A- mang the rigs wi' An- nie O.

The sky was blue, the wind was still,
The moon was shining clearly;
I set her down, wi right gude will,
Amang the rigs o' barley:
I ken't her heart was a' my ain;
I lov'd her most sincerely;
I kiss'd her o're an' o'er again,
Amang the rigs o' barley.

*Chorus*

I lock'd her in my fond embrace;
Her heart was beating rarely:
My blessings on that happy place,
Amang the rigs o' barley !
But by the moon and stars so bright,
That shone that hour so clearly !
She aye shall bless that happy night
Amang the rigs o' barley !

*Chorus*

I hae been blythe wi' comrades dear;
I hae been merry drinking;
I hae been joyfu' gath'rin gear;
I hae been happy thinking:
But a' the pleasures e'er I saw,
Tho' three times doubl'd fairly,
That happy night was worth them a',
Amang the rigs o' barley.

*Chorus*

OMB 96

# Green Grow the Rashes, O

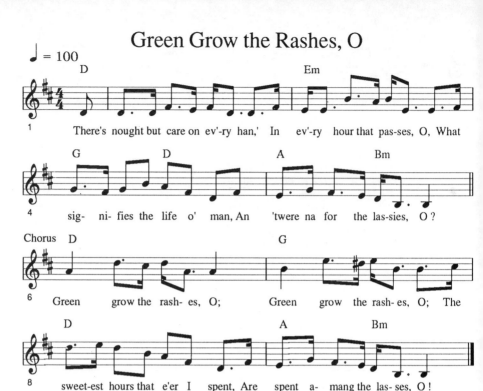

♩ = 100

There's nought but care on ev'-ry han,' In ev'-ry hour that pas-ses, O, What sig- ni- fies the life o' man, An 'twere na for the las-sies, O ?

**Chorus**

Green grow the rash- es, O; Green grow the rash- es, O; The sweet-est hours that e'er I spent, Are spent a- mang the las- ses, O !

2 The war'ly race may riches chase,
   An' riches still may fly them, O;
   An' tho' at last they catch them fast,
   Their hearts can ne'er enjoy them, O.

   *Chorus*

3 But gie me a cannie hour at e'en,
   My arms about my dearie, O;
   An' war'ly cares, an' war'ly men,
   May a' gae tapsalteerie, O !

   *Chorus*

4 For you sae douce, ye sneer at this;
   Ye're nought but senseless asses, O:
   The wisest man the warl' e'er saw,
   He dearly lov'd the lasses, O.

   *Chorus*

5 Auld Nature swears, the lovely dears
   Her noblest work she classes, O:
   Her prentice han' she try'd on man,
   An' then she made the lasses, O.

   *Chorus*

# I'm Owre Young to Marry Yet

♩ = 108
Chorus: D

I'm owre young, I'm owre young, I'm owre young to mar-ry yet; I'm owre young, t'wad be a sin, To tak' me frae my mam-mie yet. I am my mam-mie's ae bairn, Wi' un-co folk I wea-ry, sir; And ly-ing in a man's bed, I'm fley'd it mak' me ee-rie, sir.

*Chorus*

Hallowmass is come and gane,
The nights are lang in winter, sir,
And you an' I in ae bed, —
In trowth, I dare na venture, sir.

*Chorus*

Fu' loud an' shrill the frosty wind
Blaws thro' the leafless timmer, sir;
But if ye come this gate again,
I'll aulder be gin simmer, sir.

*Chorus*

OMB 96

# Flow Gently, Sweet Afton

Flow gent- ly, sweet Af- ton! a- mong thy green braes, Flow gent- ly, I'll sing thee a song in thy praise; My Ma- ry's a- sleep by thy mur- mur- ing stream, Flow gent- ly, sweet Af- ton, dis- turb not her dream.

Thou stock dove whose echo resounds thro' the glen,
Ye wild whistling blackbirds in yon thorny den,
Thou green crested lapwing, thy screaming forbear,
I charge you, disturb not my slumbering Fair.

How lofty, sweet Afton, thy neighbouring hills,
Far mark'd with the courses of clear, winding rills;
There daily I wander as noon rises high,
My flocks and my Mary's sweet cot in my eye.

How pleasant thy banks and green valleys below,
Where, wild in the woodlands, the primroses blow;
There oft, as mild Ev'ning weeps over the lea,
The sweet-scented birk shades my Mary and me.

The crustal stream, Afton, how lovely it glides,
And winds by the cot where my Mary resides;
How wanton thy waters her snowy feet lave,
As, gathering sweets flowerets, she stems thy clear wave.

Flow gently, sweet Afton, amang thy green braes,
Flow gently, sweet river, the theme of my lays;
My Mary's asleep by thy murmuring stream,
Flow gently, sweet Afton, disturb not her dream.

# Auld Lang Syne

2 And surely ye'll be your pint-stowp !
And surely I'll be mine !
And we'll tak' a cup o' kindness yet,
For auld lang syne.

*Chorus*

3 We twa hae run about the braes,
And pu'd the gowans fine;
But we've wander'd mony a weary fit
Sin' auld lang syne.

*Chorus*

4 We twa hae paidl'd in the burn,
Frae morning sun till dine;
But seas between us braid hae roar'd
Sin' auld lang syne.

*Chorus*

5 And there's a hand, my trusty fere !
And gie's a hand o' thine !
And we'll tak' a right gude willie-waught,
For auld lang syne.

*Chorus*

OMB 96

Verses intended to be written below a noble Earl's picture

Whose is that noble, dauntless brow?
 And whose that eye of fire?
And whose that generous, Princely mien,
 Ev'n rooted Foes admire?

Stranger, to justly show that brow,
 And mark that eye of fire,
Would take His hand, whose vernal tints,
 His other Works admire.

Bright as a cloudless Summer-sun,
 With stately port he moves;
His guardian Seraph eyes with awe
 The noble Ward he loves.

Among th' illustrious Scottish Sons
 That Chief thou may'st discern,
Mark Scotia's fond. returning eye,
 It dwells upon Glencairn

**Burns' Handwriting**

60

# A Brief Guide to the Songs

Although in no way meant to be comprehensive, the following notes will give as far as is relevant and traceable some idea of the background of each song in this volume.

### 9. Scots Wha Ha'e
Often regarded as the Scottish National Anthem, this song was written by Burns on August 1, 1793. In a letter to his publisher George Thomson he writes: 'There is a tradition which I have met with in many places in Scotland, that it ('Hey Tutti Tatti') was Robert Bruce's march at the battle of Bannockburn.' Burns may have been inspired by his visit to the site of the battle in 1787, when he imagined 'gallant, heroic countrymen coming o'er the hill and down upon the plunderers of their country.'

wha ha'e wi' — who have with; lour — threatening; sae — so

### 10. O Whistle and I'll Come to You My Lad
Although this tune (without its 'Scots Snap') is well-known in Ireland, it may have been composed by a John Bruse, an obscure fiddler from Dumfries around 1750. Burns wrote two sets of verses, this being the most complete version as published in Thomson's collection of 1793.

tent — take care; back-yett — gate at the back; a-jee — a-jar; syne — then; back-stile — back stairs ?; na — not; kirk — church; gang by — stay with; care'd na a flie — wouldn't hurt a fly; blink — wink/gaze; e'e — eye; a-wee — a little while; wile — beguile (steal)

### 11. Craigie-Burn Wood
Burns wrote two versions of this song. The old air which served as a basis for it lost its chorus in the process, something which was instantly welcomed by some: 'There is no need to mention the chorus. The man that would attempt to sing a chorus to this beautiful air, should have his throat cut to prevent him from doing it again!' The woods of Craigie-Burn, near Moffat, were a favourite haunt of Burns and it was here he was inspired by the amorous efforts between a local girl and his friend Mr. Gillespie to compose this song.

fa's — falls; nocht — nought/nothing; wight — chap/person; Fain — gladly; na — not; langer — longer; anither — another; frae — from

### 12. The Gloomy Night
1786 must have been one long gloomy night for Burns with much turmoil and upheavals in his personal life. Having left his (expectant) betrothed Jean Armour under pressure from her father, Burns turned to his 'Highland Mary' (Mary Campbell). He also considered emigration to Jamaica, but must have been quite depressed when Mary died unexpectedly in October. He left for Edinburgh in November of the same year. It is interesting to note that this song poem is entirely in English, it is not graced by a single Scottish word or expression.

### 14. My Tocher's the Jewel
Written for the 'Museum' in 1790. The air is roughly based on 'The mucking of Geordie's Byre'. Much in the style of 'What can a young lassie', this song examines the greedy side of

OMB 96

human nature with some bitter-sweet humour.

meikle — a lot; brawlie — well; tocher — dowry; siller — silver (money); canna — can not; hae — have; airle penny — earnest money; wad would; an — even if; maun — must; timmer — timber; frae — from; crack your credit wi' masir nor me — go bankrupt without me

### 15. To the Weaver's Gin Ye Go
One of the liveliest and sprightliest songs in this collection. Very few of Burns' sources mention this fine song and its history is quite obscure when compared against the certified masses of information relating to most of his songs and poems.

ance — once; simmer — summer; westlin' — from the West; gart — made; sang —song; gin —if/should; rede — advise; gang — go; warp — weave; wab — weft/cloth; sab — sob; thrum — purr/hum (of loom); aye — always; ca'd it roun — turned it around; gae a stoun — (lit.) gave an ache; fa' me — befall me; kintra — country

### 16. Highland Mary
Written in 1792 and thought to have been composed on the sixth anniversary of Mary Campbell's death. The tune is 'Katherine Oge'.

braes — slopes of hills; drumlie — muddy; simmer — summer; birk — beech tree; mony — many; fu' — full; aft — often; hae — have; sae — so; dwalt — dwelt

### 18. My Love she's but a Lassie Yet
The air is known as 'Lady Badinscoth's Reel' and 'Miss Farquharson's Reel'. Many other versions of the same song exist: James Hogg's song of the same title was once as popular. An altered version of Wordsworth's 'A Famous Man was Robin Hood' was also sung to the same air.

twa — two; drap — drop

### 19. The Gallant Weaver
In the early spring of 1786, Burns' love, 'bonnie Jean' was packed off by her parents to the town of Paisley. Two months later, Burns heard of his love having danced 'The Weaver's March' with a certain Robie Wilson, a weaver, to whom she was to be married. The poet was driven to distraction by this rumour, and only years later managed to write this little poetic revenge for Jean. It is interesting to note that in 'The Caledonian Museum' edition of 1809 (edited by Burn's son) this song is entered as 'The Gallant Sailor' as if to shift the attention away from any personal events in the past. The air 'The Weaver's March' is from Aird's Selection of Scots Airs' of 1784. The Cart is a small river in Renfrewshire that flows through Paisley.

rins rowin — runs rolling; aught — eight; gied — got; tocher-band — dowry; gie — give

### 20. Last May a Braw Wooer
A humorous song written in 1787 and subsequently often altered by both Burns himself as well as his publisher, Johnson. The tune is 'The Queen of the Lothians', or 'The Lothian Lassie'.

braw — fine/good; sair — sore; deave — deafen/annoy; gae — go; spak — spoke; e'en — eyes; forgie — forgive; liked — fancied; mailen — farmer; loot — let on; hae waur — have worse; wad — would; jad — jade/wild young woman; niest/neist — next; glowr'd — stared; owre/o'er — over; shouther — shoulder; spier'd — asked/inquired; fu' couthy — full loving; gin — if; shoon — shoes; schachl't — shapeless; maun — must

## 22. Gae Bring to Me a Pint O' Wine (*My Bonnie Mary*)
Allegedly written by Burns after witnessing a young officer take leave of his dearie at the pier of Leith. This song together with 'Auld Lang Syne' was sent to Burns' friend Mrs. Dunlop in December 1788, mentioning that both were old songs. Once more it seems, Burns in his search for new songs and airs came upon many fine old fragments of songs which he adapted and completed, while generally respecting the originals.

tassie — small cup; wad — would

## 23. Ye Banks and Braes
Written in 1794 to the tune of 'The Caledonian Hunt's Delight'. The story may reflect the poet's concern regarding Peggy Kennedy, the young niece of his friend Gavin Hamilton. Burns had stayed with the young girl and he wrote the song 'Young Peggy' for her. Years later on hearing of her predicament brought about by a 'false-hearted lover' he composed this song. This is possibly one of the best known of all Burns' songs.

brae — slope of a hill; aft — often; ilka — every; staw — stole

## 24. O This is No My Ain Lassie
Written in 1795. The air 'This is No My Ain House' had already been popular before Burns, in fact a wide variety of versions existed, ranging from nursery-rhymes to a Jacobite song. The Jean alluded to in the song is more than likely to have been Jean Lorimer, the daughter of a local farmer (the 'Chloris' of some of Burns' poems).

weel — well; lang — long; aye — always; sae pawkie — so crafty/shrewd; blink — gaze/glance; gleg — quick

## 26. The Birks of Aberfeldy
In 1787 Burns made a tour of the Highlands and visited the famous waterfalls of Moness, near Aberfeldy in Perthshire. The chorus of his composition is based on an existing song:
'Bonnie Lassie, will ye go
Will ye go, will ye go
Bonnie Lassie will ye go
To the Birks o' Aberfeldie?'
The air first appears in Playford's 'Dancing Master' (1657) as 'A Scotch Ayre'.

## 27. Lord Gregory
This ancient ballad is related to 'The Lass of Roch Royale', or 'The Lass of Loch Royan,' (Child 76). Burns wrote these words in 1795, to be included in Thomson's 'Collection of original Scottish Airs' (vol 1). Having read an 'improved,' rewritten version of the song from the hand of Dr. Wolcot ('Peter Pindar'), Burns furnished his own interpretation of it. 'My song, though much inferior in poetic merit, has, I think, more of the ballad simplicity in it.'

OMB 96

Although earlier folk-versions as collected by the great ballad-scholar Professor Child ran into 35 verses, Burns left us with a manageable three.

mirk — gloomy/murky; waefu' — woeful; wad — would; aye — for ever/always; flinty — keen/sharp; wrangs — wrongs

### 28. O Willie Brew'd a Peck o' Maut
A drinking song written by Burns after spending a joyous meeting near Moffat in September of 1787, with his good friends 'honest' Alan Masterton (who provided the tune) and William Nicol.

maut — malt; lee-lang — live-long; fou/fu' — full (drunk); drappie — a little drop; e'e — eye; ay — always; bree — brew/juice; trow — vow/swear; mair — more

### 30. My Love is Like a Red, Red Rose
This is what John Grieg, the editor of 'Scots Minstrelsie' has to say about this well-known song: 'Rough ore, thrown into the melting-pot of Burns's genius, comes out as purest gold.' This song is the result of a lot of improvements and changes, both in the words and the music. The original may have been written by a Lieutenant Hinches. Burns introduced parts of another 'farewell' type song. Although the poem originally was sung to the air 'Major Graham' and later to 'Queen Mary's Lament', it is nowadays married to a modern version of 'Low Down in the Broom'.

### 31. She's Fair and Fause
From the fourth volume of 'The Scots Musical Museum' of 1792. A cautionary tale of the vicissitudes of love; in this case the story of a good friend of Burns, the unfortunate Mr. Alexander Cunningham. Burns's friend was betrothed to an Edinburgh beauty, who unceremoniously dumped him when a wealthier suitor arrived. The tune is 'The Lads of Leith'.

fause — false; meikle/muckle/mickle — much/ a lot; e'en gae hang —     may even go and hang myself; coof — fool; routh o' gear — plenty of riches; hae tint — have lost; wha e'er — whoever; nae ferlie — no wonder; fa'n — fallen; 't wad been o'er meikle — it would have been too much; to gi'en thee mair — to give thee more

### 32. Tam Glen
This plaintive song of a maiden so in love with her Tam Glen was written by Burns in 1788 for Johnson's 'Museum'. Apart from the wonderful tale-telling quality of a song like this there's an added element in the references to old Scottish folklore and superstitions. The Valentine's Dealing mentioned was an old custom where on St. Valentine's Eve the lassies and lads would be drawing lots with the name of their sweethearts for the following year. Halloween in the past was surrounded with customs and odd beliefs such as the one referred to in the final stanza: 'my droukit sark-sleeve' etc. Burns himself explained this superstition: 'you go out, one or more (for this is a social spell) to a south-running spring or rivulet, where 'three lairds' lands meet, and dip your left shirt sleeve. Go to bed in sight of a fire, and hang your wet sleeve before it to dry. Lie awake; and some time near midnight, an apparition, having the exact figure of the grand object in question, will come and turn the sleeve, as if to dry the other side of it.' An old ballad with the name Tam Glen but with a different air precedes this song. Burns adopted 'The Mucking O' Geordie's Byre' as the tune.

tittie — sister; len' — lend; sic a braw — such a fine; poortith — poverty; manna — may not; Laird — Lord; ben — down; blaws — blows; siller — silver (money); minnie — mother; deave — annoy (lit. deafen); gin — if; yestreen — yesterday evening; mou' gied a sten' — mouth leapt ; drowkit —soaked; sark-sleeve — sleeve of garment; staukin — stalking; breeks — trousers; gif — if; loe — love

## 34. My Wife's a Winsome Wee Thing

The air to this song appears in Oswald's 'Caledonian Pocket Companion' (c.1755). George Thomson, Burns' publisher, suggested that Robert try his hand at some more old Scots songs and make them fit for publication. A conscientious Burns wrote back to him, providing Thomson with such improvements, but also with some valuable feeling and insights of how the poet saw the Scots song heritage and the difficult task of sensitive and sympathetic adaptation. 'If you mean my dear sir, that all the songs in your collection shall be poetry of the first merit, I am afraid you will find more difficulty in the undertaking than you are aware of. There is a peculiar rhytmus in many of our airs, and a necessity of adapting syllables to the emphasis, or what I would call the feature-notes of the tune, that cramp the poet, and lay him under almost insuperable difficulties. For instance in the air, 'My Wife's a Wanton Wee Thing', if a few lines smooth and pretty can be adapted to it, it is all you can expect. The following were made extempore to it; and though, on further study, I might give you something more profound, yet it might not suit the light-horse gallop of the air so well as this random clink.' When Thomson in spite of the foregoing took the liberty to suggest to Burns that the second stanza might be exchanged against one written by himself, Burns gracefully assented and declared it 'a positive improvement'.

neist — next; tine — to lose; warld's wrack — the end of the world (lit. the wreck of the world); warstle — wrestle; care — worries; leeze on me — you're dear to me; sae meikle mair o't — see a lot more of it; repine — fret

## 35. My Heart's in the Highlands

Burns relates that 'the first half-stanza of this song is old. The rest is mine'. The air is more than likely of Gaelic origin. Burns himself mentions 'Failte na Moise' as the source. The song itself may be based on 'The Strong Walls of Derry' the first part of which is as follows:
'The first day I landed 'twas on Irish ground
The tidings came to me from fair Derry town
That my love was married, and to my sad woe
And I lost my first love by courting too slow.'

## 36. The Deil's Awa' wi' the Exciseman

There are two conflicting stories about the origins of this song. In the first and most dramatic, Burns, the exciseman, finds himself awaiting reinforcements from Dumfries before boarding a French brig to impound her cargo. After several hours waiting in the wet salt marshes Burns was getting increasingly impatient and was heard to abuse his colleague Lewars, who had galloped off with the message. One of the waiting men suggested that devil should take Lewars for his pains and that Burns might meanwhile produce a song about the leisurely messenger. Burns allegedly said nothing, but after walking along the shore some time, returned and recited this wonderfully wicked little song. The second and more down to earth version has Burns simply writing the verses for a toast at an excisemen's dinner. It is of course possible that he first wrote it in the marshes and later recited it publicly at the dinner! The tune

OMB 96

is 'The Hemp Dresser', first printed in Playford's 'Dancing Master' of 1675.

deil — devil; ilka — every; Auld Mahoun — Old Devil (from Mohammed); mak our malt — make our malt; mony braw — many handsome/many hearty; meikle/muckle/mickle — great/big; ae best dance — best dance ever/still

### 37. What Can a Young Lassie do wi' an Auld Man?

From volume 3 of Johnson's 'Museum' of 1790. Once again an old tune to which several sets of words had been written before Burns came on the scene. A truly superb example of Burns's skill as a poet but also as someone with a perfect sense of linking the musical and poetic structures together. This is one of the songs in this collection that can really only be done justice when sung by someone familiar and comfortable with the auld Scots tongue. The internal rhyming in each first and third verse gives the words a fine jaunty feeling. The air is also used to carry the song 'The Green Purse' by Allan Ramsay.

minnie — mother; puir — poor; siller an' lan' — silver (money) and land; hosts — coughs; hirples — limps/hobbles/drags; doyl't — stupid; dozin — impotent/dopey; hankers — hangs around; dool — sorrow

### 38. There was a Lad was Born in Kyle

This song could be taken as a form of Burns's self-analysis: a poetic description of his own genius and weaknesses. The verse referring to the date of his birth shows it to be Jan, 25, 1759, last year 'but one' of the reign of King George III. The air to the first part of the song is based on an old dance tune 'The Duke of Bucclugh's tune'. The full tune is also known as 'Fiddler's Morris' in Walsh's 'Complete Country Dancing Master' of 1718. The ancestor of all these tunes is the air 'O gin ye were dead, gudeman,' which dates back to the 16th century. Although Burns wrote, in the tradition of the time, many a licentious parody of some ditties, the last verse of this song is just about the only bit of bawdiness that continued in print in practically all editions of his work.

what-na day — what day; what-na style —what way; hindmost — last/final; ane — one; janwar' win' — January wind; hansel/handsel — good-luck gift for new beginning; keekit — glanced; loof — palm of the hand; quo' scho — (quoted) said she; waly — fine/mighty; nae coof — no fool; sma' — small; aboon/abune — above; leeze me on thee — you're dear to me; ye gar — you make; lie aspar — lie with the legs apart; fauts — faults

### 40. The Highland Widow's Lament

Burns got the Gaelic air for this song from a lady in the Highlands. The substance of this dramatic song is the lamentable state of affairs in Scotland around the time of the battle of Culloden (1746). The devastation was so great that as a prophesy had earlier warned: 'her people might ride for fifty miles among her hills and valleys, and not find a reeking house, nor hear a crawing cock'. The ochon, ochon, ochrie lamentation are expressions of grief, undoubtedly contained in the original Gaelic lament.

na sae — not so; yowes — ewes; knowes — hilltops; sair, sair — woe, woe (lit. sore); brawest — best/bravest; waefu' — woeful

### 41. Wandering Willie

The air was previously published in Oswald's 'Caledonian Pocket Companion'. Burns's verses are directly based on the old song 'Here awa', there awa', here awa' Willie' first printed in Bremner's 'Scots Tunes'(1757). Burns created two sets of verses of the same songs, the second, revised version being the one that gained universal acceptance.

here awa,' there awa' — hereabouts, thereabouts; haud awa' hame — go on home; simmer — summer; ance — once

## 42. A Highland Lad my Love was Born
These verses appear posthumously in Thomson's 'Scottish Song' of 1818. They were written to the air of 'O! and Ye were Deid, Guidman,' and were also used in the cantata 'The Jolly Beggars' (probably 1785)

Lallans — Lowlands; braw — handsome; lan' — land; philibeg/philabeg/fillebeg — kilt; claymore — highlanders large two-edge sword; cann — a jar (drink)

## 44. Whistle O'er the Lave O't
Written in 1789 to replace an old song which was considered 'too coarse for publication'.

spier/speir nae mair — ask no more; o'er the lave o't — be of one mind/be friends; na — not; wha — who; maun — must/might

## 45. A Rose-bud by My Early Walk
The subject of this song was Janet (Jeannie), the daughter of William Cruickshanks, one of the masters of the High School in Edinburgh. Burns was much taken with the musical talent of young Janet and wrote these and some other verses inscribed on the blank leaf of a book which he presented to her. The air is a derivation of 'The Shepherd's Wife'.

bawk/bauk — ridge of land left untilled; tents —marks

## 46. A Man's a Man for a' That
It is known that Burns harboured republican feelings and frequently spoke in favour of the French and American Revolutions. Society and the class-system in particular was for the first time ever perceived as something unfair and to be improved upon. The great classic essay on democracy, 'The Rights of Man' by Tom Paine, was published in England in 1791. Burns own opinion of this song (written in 1794) was rather subdued: 'I fear for my songs, however, a few may please, yet originality is a coy feature in composition, and in multiplicity of efforts in the same style, disappears altogether. A great critic (Aikin) on song says, that love and wine are the exclusive themes for song-writing. The following is on neither subject, and consequently is no song, but will be allowed, I think, to be two or three pretty good prose thoughts inverted into rhyme.' The tune appears in 1759 in Bremner's 'Scots Reels' as 'Lady McIntosh's Reel'.

a' — all ; gowd — gold; hoddin grey — coarse homespun cloth; birkie — a conceited fellow; coof — fool/twit; aboon — above; maunna fa' that — must/may not do that; pith — force/strength; bear the gree — be victorious

## 48. Ae Fond Kiss
Walter Scott felt that: 'these exquisitely affecting stanzas contain the essence of a thousand

OMB 96

love tales.' It is believed that this song relates to the poet's parting with his 'Clarinda' whose real name was Mrs. Agnes McLehose and whose relationship with Burns appeared to be the only one he managed to keep platonic. The air 'Rory Dall's Port' is an ancient harp tune attributed to the blind harper Dall, who was born on the Isle of Lewis around 1600. A great deal of variants exist of this air and over the years 'Ae Fond Kiss' was - apparently by popular choice - slightly changed away from the air to which the words were set originally. One version appears in Captain Fraser's 'Collection of Airs and Melodies Peculiar to the Highlands' (1816), where it is printed as 'The Cow-Boy'. No less than three main settings of this song are doing the rounds.

ae — a; nae — no; ilka — every

## 49. Braw, Braw Lads
Written in 1792. The air appears in Oswald's 'Collection' of 1755 as 'The Brave Lads of Gallawater'. No lesser musician than Haydn declared that 'Gala Water' was his 'favourite song'.

braw — handsome; braes — slopes of hills; shaws — thicket/wood; coft — bought; ane — one; aboon — above; a' — all; lo'e — love; nae — no; laird — lord; hae — have; meikle tocher — large dowry; tent — tend/herd

## 50. Bonnie Jean (*There Was a Lass and She Was Fair*)
This was an old song that already, before Burns' time had been re-written and adapted many times. The tune 'Bonny Jean of Aberdeen' appears in Craig's 'Collection of Old Scottish Airs (1730). This is what Burns wrote to his publisher Thomson: 'I have just finished the following ballad, and, as I do think it is in my style, I send it you. Mr. Clarke, who wrote down the air from Mrs. Burns' wood-note wild, is very fond of it, and has given it a celebrity by teaching it to some young ladies of the first fashion here . . . . . the heroine of the foregoing is Miss Macmunro, daughter to Mr. Macmunro of Drumlawrig, one of your subscribers. I have not painted her in the rank which she holds in life, but in the dress and character of a cottager.'

kirk — church; aye — always; wark — coarse homespun cloth; lintwhithe — flaxen/fair; brawest — best /most handsome; owsen — oxen; naigies — small nags/horses; lang ere — long before; wist —knew; tint — lost; stourn — stolen; e'en — eyes; wad — would; weel — well; loup — leap/jump; ilka — every; lo'e —love; tent — look after; nae/na — no; twa — two

## 52. Ay Waukin', O
'Ay waukin' or 'Ay Wakin' is an old song existing in both triple and common time versions. There is conflicting evidence as to exactly what was contributed to it by Burns.

ay waukin — still awake; eerie — scared/restless; canna — can not; rins — runs; heugh — cliff/bank(of river); hame — home; lanely — lonely; bleer my e'en wi' greetin — getting my eyes bleary from weeping

## 53. Comin' Thro' the Rye
Originally published as a single sheet song before Burns 'tidied it up' and re-wrote some of the verses. Many 'indelicate' versions floated around in Burns' time.

gin — if; frae — from; ilka — every; nane — none; lo'e — love; waur — worse; hame — home; dinna — don't

## 54. Corn Rigs are Bonnie (*The Rigs o' Barley*)
Burns always felt that the last stanza of this song was the finest he had ever written; 'at least the one that pleases me best, and comes nearest my beau ideal of poetic perfection'. The tune 'Corn Rigs' is already mentioned in Playfords' 'Choice Airs' of 1631 as 'a northern song'.

Lammas — Aug 1, a Scottish quarter day; corn rigs — strips of land planted with corn; hied — went in haste; tentless — careless; sma' — small

## 56. Green Grow the Rashes O
The tune of this song has a long pedigree, going back as far as the lute book manuscript of Sir Robert Gordon of Straloch (1627), where it is found as 'Green Greus ye Rasses. A Daunce'. Both the tune and Burns's lyrics are exquisite. Once more, Burns took an old favourite ditty, regarded by decent folk as having 'indelicate' words, and re-wrote the song with superb insight into what was poetically memorable and musically natural. 'Green Grow' and 'A Man's a Man for All That' are two songs deserving to be as well-known as 'Lang Syne' for their international and timeless sentiments.

rashes — rushes; cannie/canny — quiet(ly); e'en — evening; tapsalteerie — topsy-turvy; sae douce — so kind/pleasant

## 57. I'm Owre Young to Marry Yet
Burns wrote: 'The chorus of this song is old; the rest of it, such as it is, is mine.' The tune is an anonymous Strathspey.

owre — too; 't wad — it would; tak — take; frae — from; ae bairn — only child; wi' unco — with strange; fley'd — scared; eerie — afraid/apprehensive; gane — gone; na — not; Fu' — Full; gate — way/road; aulder be gin simmer — be older by the summer

## 58. Flow Gently, Sweet Afton
This song, together with only a few others, breathes very little of the earthy Scottishness of the main body of Burns' output. The rather genteel language may be something to do with the fact that he was nearly embarrassed with gratefulness towards a Mrs. Stewart of Afton, in Ayrshire, who was the first person of high station to recognize his genius. The song (1786) was dedicated to Mrs. Stewart, but the 'Slumbering Fair' of the song is likely to have been his own beloved 'Highland Mary', whom he courted in that year. Generally, this song has a lot in common with the type of songs Thomas Moore (who was roughly a contemporary) fashioned out of old Irish airs.

braes — slopes of hills; birk — beech tree

## 60. Auld Lang Syne
Although Burns is generally credited with this song, he only added the third and fourth verses to an already existing song of the same name. Burns wrote: 'The air is but mediocre; but the following song, the old song of the olden times and which has never been in print, nor even in manuscripts, until I took it down from an old man's singing, is enough to recommend any air.'

OMB 96

Thomson, Burns' publisher, set the words to another better-fitting air: 'I fee'd a lad at Michaelmas', also known as 'The Miller's Wedding', 'The Miller's Daughter', and 'Sir Alexander Don's Strathspey'. Although 'Lang Syne' owes much to the literary and musical intercessions of Burns and Thomson, it continues to shine and charm us with its timeless simplicity. Some songs always engender this warm feeling of being there because we needed them. If Silent Night produces that same feeling at Christmas time, 'Lang Syne' will do this on New Year's Eve all around the world and more particularly at Scottish gatherings.

auld lang syne — of long ago/lit. 'old long since' ; pint-stoup — pint-size tankard; brae — the side of a hill; pu'd — pulled; gowans — daisies; mony — many; paid'led — paddled; dine — dinner-time; braid — broad; hae — have; fiere — friend/companion; gie's — give us; gude — good; willie-waught — draught (of drink)

# BIBLIOGRAPHY

*The English Dancing Master*, Playford 17th cent.
*Choice Airs*, Playford 1631
*Ancient and Modern Scottish Songs, Heroic Ballads, etc.*, David Herd 18th cent.
*Complete Country Dancing Master*, Walsh, 1718
*A Collection of the Choicest Scots Tunes adapted for the Harpsichord or Spinet*, Adam Craig, Edinburgh, 1730
*A Collection of Curious Scots Tunes*, James Oswald, 1742
*The Caledonian Pocket Companion*, James Oswald, (12 Vols.) c.1742-1760
*Collection of Scots Tunes*, Bremner, 1757
*A Selection of Scotch, English, Irish & Foreign Airs adapted to the Fife, Violin or German Flute*, by Jas. Aird, Glasgow (6 books) c.1775-1800
*The Scots National Museum*, James Johnson, (6 vols.) 1787-1803
*Caledonian Museum*, Johnson 1790
*Scottish Songs*, Thomson 1793, 1795 & 1818
*The Caledonian Musical Museum*, J. Dick, London, 1809
*The English & Scottish Popular Ballads*, ed. F.J. Child (5 vols.) 1882-1894, republished by Dover Publications, New York
*Minstrelsy of Scotland*, A. Moffat, Augener, 1895
*The Poetry of Robert Burns*, (4 vols) edited by W.E. Henley and T. F. Henderson, Caxton, London, 1896.
*The Songs of Burns*, J.K. Lees, Bayley & Ferguson, Glasgow 1896
*A History of Music in Scotland*, H.G. Farmer, Hinrichsen, London 1947?
*The Complete Illustrated Poems, Songs and Ballads of R. Burns*, J.M. Dent & Co. 1965
*The Traditional and National Music of Scotland*, F. Collinson, Routledge & Kegan Paul, London 1966
*A History of Scottish Music*, K. Elliot & F. Rimmer, BBC 1973
*Poems and Songs*, Robert Burns, Gordon Wright Publishing, Edinburgh 1978
*Scotland's Music*, C.T. Davie, W. Blackwood, Edinburgh 1980
*Scottish Traditional Music*, N. Wood, Chambers, Edinburgh 1991
*The Songs of Robert Burns*, J.C. Dick, n.d.
*Lyric Gems of Scotland*, John Cameron, Glasgow, n.d.
*Scots Minstrelsie*, John Greig, Jack, Edinburgh n.d.
*Scots Reels*, Bremner, n.d.

## DISCOGRAPHY

*Songs of Robert Burns*, sung by Ewan MacColl, Ossian, Cork, 1994.
*Robert Burns in Poetry, Song and Prose*, Arnold Johnson, Peerless, Middlesex, 1973
*The Songs of Robert Burns*, Jean Redpath, arr, Serge Hovey, Greentrax, Edinburgh (in progress)
*Love Songs of Robert Burns*, Ann Moray, Spoken Arts Inc. USA, 1987
*Songs of Robert Burns*, sung by Andy M. Stewart, Green Linnet, USA.
*The Robert Burns Songbook* Bill McCue, Helen McArthur, Peter Morrison and David Solley, Lismor
*To Robert Burns, A Tribute* Kenneth McKellar, Lismor